5/05 1* 5/04

LOS GATOS PUBLIC LIBRARY
P.O. BOX 949
Los Gatos, CA 95031
408 354-6891

CANADA GOOSE

Life Cycles

Jason Cooper

Rourke
Publishing LLC
Vero Beach, Florida 32964

www.rourkepublishing.com

PHOTO CREDITS: All photos © Lynn M. Stone

Cover: *Canada geese often rest on water after eating on land.*

Editor: Frank Sloan

Cover and page design by Nicola Stratford

Library of Congress Cataloging-in-Publication Data

Cooper, Jason, 1942-
  Canada goose / Jason Cooper.
     p. cm. — (Life cycles)
Summary: Describes the physical characteristics, behavior, habitat, and life cycle of the Canada goose, with an emphasis on the hatching and raising of its young.
Includes bibliographical references (p.   ).
  ISBN 1-58952-351-2 (hardcover)
  1. Canada goose—Juvenile literature. [1. Canada goose. 2. Geese. 3. Animals—Infancy.] I. Title.
  QL696.A52 C664 2002
  598.4'178—dc21
                                                                      2002006228
Printed in the USA

CG/CG

Table of Contents

A Canada goose bobs to grab underwater plant pieces.

Canada Geese

Canada geese are big, brownish birds with long necks and webbed feet. They like to swim and **bob** for water plants. But they like to eat corn in fields and grass on lawns, too.

Canada geese live throughout much of North America, not just in Canada. They are called Canada geese because they were first discovered there.

Goslings

Several kinds of wild geese have life cycles very much like that of Canada geese. That cycle starts with baby geese, called **goslings**.

A Canada goose incubates eggs on her nest, built on top of a muskrat lodge.

A gosling dries on a warm, early July day in Canada's Arctic region.

Geese hatch from eggs, as all birds do. A mother goose lays about five eggs in a soft nest made of plants and soft feathers. Her nest is usually on the ground.

A male goose, called a gander, stands guard behind its mate at their nest.

The mother **incubates** her eggs for 24 to 30 days. The father goose stands guard nearby.

Like other baby birds, a gosling has a small, horn-like egg tooth on its upper bill. It's not really a tooth, but it's hard and fairly sharp. A gosling cracks open the egg by chipping with its egg tooth against the shell. The gosling may hammer away for more than a day to break the egg open!

Damp and tired, goslings wriggle to free themselves from eggshells.

The gosling is damp and tired when it wriggles free from the shell. It rests under its mother's breast feathers and quickly dries.

A Covering of Down

When the tiny, soft feathers dry, they cover the gosling in a warm coat of yellow **down**. Within a few hours after hatching, a gosling is as bright-eyed and fluffy as a bunny.

In its yellow coat of down, a gosling dries in an unusual one-egg nest.

Geese are among the birds that feed themselves shortly after birth.

Many other birds are helpless after they hatch. Baby pelicans and herons, for example, stay in or by their nests. The parents bring food to them for several weeks until they are old enough to fly.

Three days old, a gosling gamely follows its parents on the tundra of the Canadian Arctic.

Out of the Nest

Goslings, however, leave the nest within 24 hours. They can't fly, but they can run along with their parents on the ground. The parents lead the goslings to food. They also protect them from **predators**, such as bobcats.

This gosling's stiff adult feathers have begun to replace its down.

Growing Up

Goslings hatch in the spring. There are plenty of fresh green plants and insects to eat in springtime.

Goslings grow quickly. Their downy feathers are soon replaced by stiffer, stronger feathers. Canada geese can fly by the time they are six to nine weeks old. Canada geese from the North fly sooner because they have longer daylight hours in which to feed.

Migration

Some flocks of Canada geese **migrate**. They often fly in a V shape. The nesting areas of these geese become snowy and icy in the winter.

This flock of migrating Canada geese is in V formation.

Migrating Canada geese stop to feed in a field where corn kernels remain after harvest.

The geese fly south each fall to find places with food and open water.

Each spring the geese fly north to nest. Young geese learn the route from their parents.

Adult pairs of wild geese often remain together for several seasons or even life.

The Life Cycle Goes On

The goose family stays together through the summer, fall, winter, and part of the following spring. But before the nesting season, the male goose forces the young geese away.

By the end of their second or third winter, young geese find a mate. The new pair usually returns to the area where the female was born. There they will nest and start a family of their own.

Stage 1: A Canada goose lays her eggs in a soft nest and incubates them.

Stage 2: When the eggs hatch, small geese, known as goslings, are born.

Stage 4: By the end of two to three seasons, the geese are fully grown and will find a mate.

Stage 3: Goslings can fly when they are six to nine weeks old.

Glossary

bob (BAHB) — to dip the head into water so that the tail rises up, like a seesaw

down (DOUN) — the soft covering of baby feathers, especially in ducks, geese, and swans

goslings (GOZ lingz) — baby geese

incubate (INK you bait) — to keep eggs warm; to develop and grow within an egg

migrate (MY grait) — to make a long, seasonal journey at the same time each year

predators (PRED uh terz) — animals that catch and eat other animals for food

Index

Further Reading

Miller, Sara S. *Waterfowl: From Swans to Screamers.* Franklin Watts, 1999

Wexo, John Bonnett. *Ducks, Geese, and Swans.* The Creative Company, 1999

Websites to Visit

http://www.bcadventure.com/adventure/wilderness/birds/index.html
http://www.ducks.ca/naturenotes/cangoose.html

About the Author

Jason Cooper has written several children's books about a variety of topics for Rourke Publishing, including recent series *China Discovery* and *American Landmarks*. Cooper travels widely to gather information for his books. Two of his favorite travel destinations are Alaska and the Far East.